Counseling Pr

CHRISTIAN

Beliefs

AN INTEGRATED APPROACH

one-time
online
access
code
included

Kendall Hunt
publishing company

DENISE
DANIEL

www.kendallhunt.com
Send all inquiries to:
4050 Westmark Drive
Dubuque, IA 52004-1840

Copyright © 2020 by Kendall Hunt Publishing Company

ISBN: 978-1-7924-1130-4

Published in the United States of America

To Aggie Johnson, LPC, LMFT
Mentor, friend, and model for living by principle

Contents

1

An Introduction to Christian Professional Counselor Identity and Principles

Beginning a professional counseling program is an exciting journey. Students often come with a mixed bag of long-awaited dreams of being a counselor and a bit of backroom lingering concern about being able to be successful. Most students have chosen the counseling profession because somewhere in their past they have either been helped by a professional

counselor themselves, or, they have had some experience in the helping professions field. But, by far, almost all students come with some preconceived ideas about the profession of counseling. And, if that student identifies themselves as a Christian, the student comes with some ideas of how one's personal beliefs can fit into the counseling relationship. All of this reflects the assumptions that beginning counselors bring to the counseling setting as they embark on a new career.

© topperspix/Shutterstock.com

The most common assumptions center on several themes:

- Who professional counselors are and are not (Identity)
- What counselors actually do (Role)
- How one's Christian theology can be used in the counseling relationship (Integration)

© Trueffelpix/Shutterstock.com

Clarifying Professional Counselor Identity

One of the first tasks given to Counselor Educators is to assist beginning professional counseling students in learning about their professional identity. This begins with understanding some of the common differences that exist between and among the mental health professions.

Besides professional counseling, there are several helping professions that comprise the mental health arena. Among these are the professions of psychiatry, psychology, social work, nursing, addictions, marriage and family therapy, and more. One of the first tasks of the beginning professional counseling student is the development of a strong professional counselor identity so that the student can clearly articulate who one is and what one does.

But, beginning counselors often struggle with understanding some fundamental differences that exist between different helping professions. The most common misunderstanding surrounds the professions of psychology and counseling. Students are often surprised to learn that a "psychologist" is not a "counselor" and vice versa; that both professional titles represent two separate professions. Psychologists are part of the psychology profession that has its' own professional association (the American Psychological Association), code of ethics, and state laws that govern what one can and cannot do under the title of "Psychologist" (Gale & Austin, 2003; Mellin, Hunt, & Nichols, 2011).

The same is true for the profession of counseling, which has its' own professional association (the American Counseling Association [ACA]), code of ethics, and state laws that govern what one can and cannot do under, unfortunately, a plethora of titles that vary from state to state. For example, "counselors" may be defined and referred to as "Licensed Professional Counselors" in one state and defined and referred to as "Licensed Mental Health Counselors" in another state. In fact, across the 50 states, there are some six different titles for licensed counselors currently in use. One can immediately see the confusion for both the counselor in training, much less, the consumer (Gale & Austin, 2003; Mellin et al., 2011; Tarvydas, Hartley, & Gerald, 2016; Wheeler, 2015).

The confusion around the title and function of a professional counselor is because the profession of counseling is a young profession currently in the process of defining its' role among a variety of mental health professions. This is part of the confusion that surrounds titles, educational requirements, licensure laws, and more. Recognizing the confusion, in 2005 the ACA made it a priority to begin the long, arduous task of defining the profession and unifying it under one title, set of educational requirements and licensure laws (Kaplan & Gladding, 2011; Leahy, Rak, & Zanskas, 2016).

For the Christian entering the professional counseling field, the confusion is compounded as students must come to realize that there is also a difference between a "Licensed Professional Counselor" and "Pastoral Counselor" that directly impacts what one can and cannot do under these titles. One of the largest, though no longer absolute, differences between a pastoral and "licensed" professional counselor is just that: states largely do not license pastoral counselors. Historically, states have stayed away from mandating religions and religious matters. However, more recently, states are beginning to require licensure for pastoral counselors. Part of this is an effort to ensure quality of mental healthcare to state citizens while meeting increasing demand for mental health services (Brammer, 2014).

There is also a difference in educational requirements. All 50 states require at least a master's degree to be eligible for licensure as a professional counselor. Additionally, all states mandate both the type and number of course hours that make up the degree. In contrast, pastoral counselors do not have any required number or type of counseling courses they must have completed to call themselves a pastoral counselor. Nor do they have a minimal entry level of education. So, a pastoral counselor can have no courses in counseling and no degree but call themselves a "Pastoral Counselor" (Sullivan, 2014; Walker, Scheidegger, End, & Amundsen, 2012).

Clarifying Professional Counselor Role

In addition to clarifying identity, beginning students must also clarify role. Many beginning students of the profession envision the work of a counselor as that of one who wisely and benevolently dispenses advice to confused clients whose problems will resolve once the advice is followed. In addition to dispensing wise advice, many beginning counselors, who also identify themselves as Christians, imagine themselves dispensing additional passages from the Bible that will instruct and edify the client sitting before them.

For beginning professional counselors, a type of "unlearning," or deconstruction, of these assumptions must occur before a realistic view of counselor identity and role can begin to form that reflects the truth of the profession. For example, becoming a professional counselor means the counseling student must move from seeing oneself as a wise sage to more of an advocate for the client.

The American Counseling Association (2014), which is the professional organization for counselors, defines the role of counseling as, ". . . a professional relationship that empowers diverse individuals, families, and groups to accomplish mental health, wellness, education, and career goals" (p. 3). As the definition emphasizes, the focus of counseling centers more on wellness than on psychopathology and prevention rather than intervention (Mellin et al., 2011).

Clarifying Responsibilities Surrounding Principles

While beginning Christian counselor trainees are navigating the new waters of unlearning and learning that centers on identity and role, a new crisis quickly emerges when they encounter the profession's stance on values. In the 2014 revision of the ACA's code of ethics, the profession issued a new directive regarding the personal values of the counselor:

> Counselors are aware of—and avoid imposing—their own values, attitudes, beliefs, and behaviors. Counselors respect the diversity of clients, trainees, and research participants and seek training in areas in which they are at risk of imposing their values onto clients, especially when the counselor's values are inconsistent with the client's goals or are discriminatory in nature (A.4.b).

In addition to this directive, the American Counseling Association (2014) took the additional step of closing the back door of referring clients due to value differences:

> Counselors refrain from referring prospective and current clients based solely on the counselor's personally held values, attitudes, beliefs, and behaviors. Counselors respect the diversity of clients and seek training in areas in which they are at risk of imposing their values onto clients, especially when the counselor's values are inconsistent with the client's goals or are discriminatory in nature (A.11.b).

The implications of these two directives are clear. Counselors may not impose their own values and beliefs upon clients, may not refer clients due to these differences, and must, instead, seek training in how to work with clients of different values, attitudes, beliefs, and behaviors. This stance came about in response to several incidents of litigation surrounding counselors, and counselors in training, refusal to counsel clients whose values conflicted with the counselor. For example, in several cases, counselors in training refused to counsel a homosexual client due to value differences (Herlihy, Hermann, & Greden, 2014).

Being backed into what can feel like a corner, beginning Christian counselors often remark to me that the solution is for the Christian counselor to work in a "Christian" setting. Though this might seem like a viable solution, I have found this does not work. Having worked in Christian settings myself, it has been my experience that one finds the same value differences in the Christian setting as the secular. For example, the fact that Protestantism has so many denominations is just one example of the differences in beliefs and values that exist within the Protestant camp.

The profession of counseling does attempt to assist counselors in navigating the issue of personal values in the counselor–client relationship. Recent literature from experts in the field have centered on learning the skill of "bracketing." Bracketing occurs when the professional counselor lays aside her own values in respect for the client's right to make his own choices. It begins with the counselor being aware that her own values are being triggered but purposefully puts personal values aside to work collaboratively with the client, not counselor, defined goals (Kocet & Herlihy, 2014).

It is at this point that beginning Christian professional counselors begin to wonder if professional counseling is really the best career choice. I think it is important to ask that question, especially at the beginning of one's education. *"If I can't refuse to see clients, or refer clients, whose values conflict with my own, and I can't bring my own values to the professional relationship, then, as a Christian, can I, and how do I, work within those parameters?"*

This is not a question that all Christians may ask themselves. However, this question often originates from the evangelical camp of Christianity. Many evangelical Christians feel responsible to fulfill the command of Christ:

> Then Jesus came to them and said, "All authority in heaven and on earth has been given to me. Therefore, go and make disciples of all nations, baptizing them in the name of the Father and of the Son and of the Holy Spirit" (Matthew 28:18-19).

For many evangelicals, this mandate infers that making disciples must exhibit itself as a purposeful, direct approach in verbally presenting the Gospel at all opportunities. For this population to not take such a direct approach often feels like disobedience to God and a personal failure of faith.

Finding an Answer through Integration

As awareness increases for beginning Christian professional counseling students, they begin to see future potential scenarios where counselor personal values might conflict with future client values. For example, questions of, "Would I be comfortable with providing relationship counseling to a gay couple?" or, "If a pregnant woman wanted to discuss her desire to have an abortion, could I support her regardless of what I value?" become all too real and possible.

© RossHelen/Shutterstock.com

The answer to this dilemma, and the premise of this book, is that the ability to hold to one's personal beliefs and values without imposing them is possible, modeled by the approach of Christ himself, and can leave the beginning Christian counselor with a measure of comfort and integrity in knowing that to do so is to honor the commands of God. To this end, this book begins at the intersection of professional principles and Christian theology.

The ACA Principles

In the preamble of the 2014 code of ethics, the ACA identifies six core principles that serve the purpose of guiding the licensed professional counselor in ethical decision-making. Not only do these principles guide counselors in navigating ethical dilemmas, at a more fundamental level, the principles are the basis for competent and compassionate care:

- Autonomy, or fostering the right to control the direction of one's life;

- Nonmaleficence, or avoiding actions that cause harm;

- Beneficence, or working for the good of the individual and society by promoting mental health and well-being;

- Justice, or treating individuals equitably and fostering fairness and equality;

- Fidelity, or honoring commitments and keeping promises, including fulfilling one's responsibilities of trust in professional relationships; and

- Veracity, or dealing truthfully with individuals with whom counselors come into professional contact (American Counseling Association, 2014, p. 3).

The purpose of this book is not to provide an in-depth look at professional counselor identity and ethics. Rather, this book exists for the beginning Christian professional counseling student to assist with the beginning task of integrating Christian beliefs with the principles of a secular profession. This book will explore each of these professional principles and how they reflect both theological truth and the life of Christ. In so doing, hopefully, the beginning Christian professional counselor will find the road to developing a professional identity and integrating into the profession of counseling an easier one.

2   Autonomy

Like so much of the rest of American society, our work culture lives and breathes by common values that keep us functioning in order rather than chaos and anarchy. For example, as a culture we value justice and equality in everything from personal relationships, to business deals, to politics. So, it is with our profession of counseling. In the preamble of the ethics code for the American Counseling Association (ACA, 2014), the profession has identified several core principles, that when looked at from the lens of a Christian, are something we can recognize as familiar: autonomy, nonmaleficence, beneficence, justice, fidelity, and veracity.

© SergioVas/Shutterstock.com

These six core values are at the heart of the profession and certainly should be at the heart of every ethically practicing professional counselor. They are road signs that assist with navigating through difficult clinical situations and ethical dilemmas. More importantly, they are the basis of compassionate care and congruent with the same behavior both taught in the Bible and modeled by God's actions throughout history.

© Lightspring/Shutterstock.com

Autonomy refers to the counselor's respect of client choices. Autonomy means clients have the right to decide their own fate about all aspects of life whether I as a counselor approve or disapprove of that decision.

Autonomy is what God exercised when He allowed Adam and Eve to make a decision that had both immediate and long-term, permanent consequences. Genesis, chapter three, unfolds the story of their choice to disobey God, willfully and knowingly reaping the consequences of sin. Yet, God is there and allows them the autonomy to make the decision.

Why would God allow such autonomy to run amok? The relationship that God desires of us is not one of obligation and duty. He has since our creation allowed us to be creatures with some sort of autonomy. He desires relationship with us, but never forces Himself upon us. Our choice is clear in many passages from the Bible where God invites us, not forces us, into relationship with Himself.

"Come, all you who are thirsty, come to the waters; and you who have no money, come, buy and eat!" is an open invitation from God to anyone who has ever waken up to a felt need and the knowledge that I am not powerful enough to meet that need (Isaiah 55:1). "Here I am! I stand at the door and knock. If anyone hears my voice and opens the door, I will come in and eat with that person, and they with me," implies I have the choice to come to the door, to open the door or not, and to invite God into my life and affairs (Revelation 3:20).

As Christian professional counselors, allowing my client the right to make their own decisions is compassion. It is both respectful and empowering. It communicates to the client my utmost trust in their abilities, sending the message that I am both aware and respectful of appropriate boundaries. As James Olthuis (2001, p. 63) has noted, "The fact that love—God's

compassionate love—is astir and aflutter in the world is of tremendous significance for a therapist. First of all, it lifts from us the impossible burden of concocting a cure." God's love for us is a mature love that recognizes that true love always is a love that is born of choice. Even at a less intimate level, no one wants someone to "have" to be in relationship with us. Instead, we desire others to "want" to be in relationship with us. It is the exercise of the choice of another that makes us feel valued.

In addition to providing space for choice, the Bible infers a collaborative relationship between the Christian and God:

> Therefore, my dear friends, as you have always obeyed—not only in my presence, but now much more in my absence—continue to work out your salvation with fear and trembling, for it is God who works in you to will and to act in order to fulfill his good purpose (Philippians 2:12-13).

This verse not only implies that there is a collaborative relationship between God and I where we work together on a common goal of my redemption, but in many ways is a glimpse into the experience of the client. As a professional counselor, I too, work in collaboration with my client in establishing and accomplishing the goals of my client for their personal growth.

Perhaps the best picture of how God allows autonomy in our lives is Jesus' parable of the prodigal son.

> [11] Jesus continued: There was a man who had two sons. [12] The younger one said to his father, 'Father, give me my share of the estate.' So, he divided his property between them. [13] Not long after that, the younger son got together all he had, set off for a distant country and there squandered his wealth in wild living. [14] After he had spent everything, there was a severe famine in that whole country, and he began to be in need. [15] So he went and hired himself out to a citizen of that country, who sent him to his fields to feed pigs. [16] He longed to fill his stomach with the pods that the pigs were eating, but no one gave him anything. [17] When he came to his senses, he said, 'How many of my father's hired servants have food to spare, and here I am starving to death! [18] I will set out and go back to my father and say to him: Father, I have sinned against heaven and against you. [19] I am no longer worthy to be called your son; make me like one of your hired servants.' [20] So he got up and went to his father. But while he was still a long way off, his father saw him and was filled with compassion for him; he ran to his son, threw his arms around him and kissed him. [21] The son said to him, 'Father, I have sinned against heaven and against you. I am no longer worthy to be called your son.' [22] But the father said to his servants, 'Quick! Bring the best robe and put it on him. Put a ring on his finger and sandals on his feet. [23] Bring the fattened calf and kill it. Let's have a feast and celebrate. [24] For this son of mine was dead and is alive again; he was lost and is found.' So they began to celebrate (Luke 15).

In ancient culture, for a son to ask for his inheritance before his father's death was considered immensely disrespectful (Longman, 2014). Yet, in the telling of this story, Jesus message is clear—the Father bears both his son's disrespect and his impeding disastrous decision. The son's foolish decision leads down the road toward destruction until the son finds himself financially, emotionally, and morally bankrupt.

The father's willingness to allow his son to make his own choices was about love. The apostle Paul reminds us that, "Love bears all things, believes all things, hopes all things, endures all things" (I Corinthian 13:7). From the depths of love, the father bears the burden of allowing his son to exercise autonomy, while simultaneously holding hope for his son's redemption.

© Suzanne Tucker/Shutterstock.com

As a Christian professional counselor, I, too, hold respect for client's choices in one hand, and hope in the redemptive power of God in the other. My hope, like the father of the prodigal son, is that God is bigger than all of our worst decisions and can use any disaster for our growth and redemption.

Name: _____   Date: _____

Scenario 1:

James is a counselor working at an addiction outpatient facility. He has been seeing Mary, a cocaine addict, with 2 months of sobriety. James believes that Mary, in addition to her addiction, also may have bipolar disorder. He informs her of his suspicion and tells her that he wants her to see a psychiatrist for diagnosis and medication. Mary refuses. Upon refusal, James tells Mary that if she does not agree to see the psychiatrist, he will refuse to continue seeing her as a client. How has James violated the principle of autonomy?

3 Nonmaleficence

Nonmaleficence is the second principle of our profession (American Counseling Association, 2014). It is the directive to "do no harm" to those who put their trust in our abilities. Nonmaleficence requires that I am responsible to act with competence and in the best interest of my client.

Trust

© Creative Stall/Shutterstock.com

Nonmaleficence also means I always use my power for my client. In the professional counseling relationship, power always belongs to the counselor, whether she recognizes it or not. This is because the counselor is the one who holds the knowledge, training, skills, and license. As much as I want it to be an equal relationship that empowers my client, I must always keep in mind that I am the one holding the power. What I do with that power becomes very important. "Will I use it for my client or for myself?" becomes an important question each professional counselor must ask himself.

© rudall30/Shutterstock.com

Like autonomy, the nonmaleficence of God springs from the depth of his love for us. He is 100% for us and is reflected in the Psalmist's words:

> Whoever dwells in the shelter of the Most High will rest in the shadow of the Almighty. [2] I will say of the Lord, "He is my refuge and my fortress, my God, in whom I trust." [3] Surely he will save you from the fowler's snare and from the deadly pestilence. [4] He will cover you with his feathers, and under his wings you will find refuge; his faithfulness will be your shield and rampart. [5] You will not fear the terror of night, nor the arrow that flies by day, [6] nor the pestilence that stalks in the darkness, nor the plague that destroys at midday. [7] A thousand may fall at your side, ten thousand at your right hand, but it will not come near you. [8] You will only observe with your eyes and see the punishment of the wicked (Psalm 51).

Like a faithful, loving father, he uses his power for our benefit. "[11] For I know the plans I have for you," . . . "plans to prosper you and not to harm you, plans to give you hope and a future," declares the Lord to the nation of Israel (Jeremiah 29:11).

Power "for" is what Adam and Eve receive when they are found hiding from God in the Garden of Eden having just willfully disobeyed God. Their behavior tells on them. They are expecting what they deserve—judgment. But, once again, God chooses a different road.

> [6] When the woman saw that the fruit of the tree was good for food and pleasing to the eye, and also desirable for gaining wisdom, she took some and ate it. She also gave some to her husband, who was with her, and he ate it. [7] Then the eyes of both of them were opened, and they realized they were naked; so they sewed fig leaves together and made coverings for themselves. [8] Then the man and his wife heard the sound of the LORD God as he was walking in the garden in the cool of the day, and they hid from the LORD God among the trees of the garden. [9] But the LORD God called to the man, "Where are you?" [10] He answered, "I heard you in the garden, and I was afraid because I was naked; so I hid."

Cowering under the brush of the garden, Adam is called out by God with one pointed question: "Where are you?" This is not a question inquiring about physical location. It is a deeper question inquiring of the state of Adam's soul. It is not a question for God's sake, but a question for Adam's sake. God desires Adam to stop and consider the present state of his relationship with God and what Adam has done.

Adam and Eve are cowering for good reason. They have violated the one command of God to not eat of the tree of the knowledge of good and evil. Further, they both have been warned that the consequences of doing so will certainly result in death (Genesis 2:17). They know they are guilty.

Their confession of hiding reveals the fear they are feeling deep within their souls. Their fear tells us they are expecting a God who is coming with a big stick of judgment. By the letter of the law, God has the right to exercise, or allow, the consequences that he clearly laid out would happen. Yet, this is a God who whose love is everlasting, immutable, and never fails. This is a God who desires, above all, our good. He does not come to harm, but, instead, chooses to do no harm.

At the question of, "Where are you?" Adam tests the loving-kindness of God and Eve quickly follows. Both respond by blaming others instead of taking responsibility for their decisions and actions.

> [9] But the LORD God called to the man, "Where are you?" [10] He answered, "I heard you in the garden, and I was afraid because I was naked; so I hid." [11] And he said, "Who told you that you were naked? Have you eaten from the tree that I commanded you not to eat from?" [12] The man said, "The woman you put here with me—she gave me some fruit from the tree, and I ate it." [13] Then the LORD God said to the woman, "What is this you have done?" The woman said, "The serpent deceived me, and I ate."

Yet, God remains patient with them. He exercises His loving-kindness and mercy by not administering the death penalty that have rightfully incurred (Genesis 2:16-17). Instead, from mercy God first lays out for them the long-term consequences of their sin and banishes them from the Garden of Eden so that they will not live eternally in a state of sin. It is a severe mercy.

As a Christian professional counselor, I am responsible to use my power in a way that does no harm for my client. Instead, as theologian Henri Nouwen (1993) has noted, I must choose to abandon power for love, again and again.

Name: _____   **Date:** _____

Scenario 2:

Carter is a counselor is a church-based setting who has been seeing Jose, a 24-year-old male. Initially, Jose presented wanting to talk about concerns at his place of employment. After eight sessions, Jose hesitantly reveals to Carter that he is gay and would like Carter to help him with his relationship with his partner. Carter refuses, stating that because he does not support the gay lifestyle, he cannot, in good conscious help Jose with his relationship. In response, Jose tears up and walks out of the session. How has Carter violated the principle of nonmaleficence?

4 Beneficence

To counsel from the principle of beneficence means I am always promoting the good of my client and the good of society (American Counseling Association, 2014). It is the one core principle that takes me beyond just the client sitting in front of me. It requires me to see my client in the context of their world and moves me to change and advocacy on behalf of my client.

Seeing my client as part of a larger system is important to understanding my client. We are more than just the sum of our parts. We are the result of the additions, subtractions, and divisions of our lives. To love my client well means I put that love into action to help my client within their systems and communities. This is the heart of the meaning of beneficence. "Do not withhold good from those to whom it is due, when it is in your power to act," says the writer of Proverbs (3:27).

> [35] 'For I was hungry and you gave me something to eat, I was thirsty and you gave me something to drink, I was a stranger and you invited me in, [36] I needed clothes and you clothed me, I was sick and you looked after me, I was in prison and you came to visit me.' [37] Then the righteous will answer him, 'Lord, when did we see you hungry and feed you, or thirsty and give you something to drink? [38] When did we see you a stranger and invite you in, or needing clothes and clothe you? [39] When did we see you sick or in prison and go to visit you?' [40] The King will reply, 'Truly I tell you, whatever you did for one of the least of these brothers and sisters of mine, you did for me' (Matthew 25).

In the world of Jesus, there is no gap between loving and doing. Love is a verb that compels us to act for the good of my clients. Additionally, my exercise of beneficence is not contingent on the attitude or worthiness of my client. It is something I give without demanding a return.

Beneficence, like love, is a one-way street running toward and for the client. It does not wait until the client's values and beliefs line up with my own. It demands, instead, that, "[3] Greater love has no one than this: to lay down one's life for one's friends" (John 15:13).

Beneficence, like love, is costly. This is the very work and message of the cross. "⁸ But God demonstrates his own love for us in this: While we were still sinners, Christ died for us," writes Paul to remind us that love came to our worlds and not the other way around (Romans 5:8).

Jesus exercised beneficence by elevating the status of those who were disenfranchised, as seen in his interaction with the woman at the well.

> ⁴ Now he had to go through Samaria. ⁵ So he came to a town in Samaria called Sychar, near the plot of ground Jacob had given to his son Joseph.⁶ Jacob's well was there, and Jesus, tired as he was from the journey, sat down by the well. It was about noon. ⁷ When a Samaritan woman came to draw water, Jesus said to her, "Will you give me a drink?" ⁸ (His disciples had gone into the town to buy food.) ⁹ The Samaritan woman said to him, "You are a Jew and I am a Samaritan woman. How can you ask me for a drink?" (For Jews do not associate with Samaritans.[a]) ¹⁰ Jesus answered her, "If you knew the gift of God and who it is that asks you for a drink, you would have asked him and he would have given you living water." ¹¹ "Sir," the woman said, "you have nothing to draw with and the well is deep. Where can you get this living water? ¹² Are you greater than our father Jacob, who gave us the well and drank from it himself, as did also his sons and his livestock?" ¹³ Jesus answered, "Everyone who drinks this water will be thirsty again, ¹⁴ but whoever drinks the water I give them will never thirst. Indeed, the water I give them will become in them a spring of water welling up to eternal life." ¹⁵ The woman said to him, "Sir, give me this water so that I won't get thirsty and have to keep coming here to draw water." ¹⁶ He told her, "Go, call your husband and come back." ¹⁷ "I have no husband," she replied. Jesus said to her, "You are right when you say you have no husband.¹⁸ The fact is, you have had five husbands, and the man you now have is not your husband. What you have just said is quite true." ¹⁹ "Sir," the woman said, "I can see that you are a prophet. ²⁰ Our ancestors worshiped on this mountain, but you Jews claim that the place where we must worship is in Jerusalem." ²¹ "Woman," Jesus replied, "believe me, a time is coming when you will worship the Father neither on this mountain nor in Jerusalem. ²² You Samaritans worship what you do not know; we worship what we do know, for salvation is from the Jews. ²³ Yet a time is coming and has now come when the true worshipers will worship the Father in the Spirit and in truth, for they are the kind of worshipers the Father seeks. ²⁴ God is spirit, and his worshipers must worship in the Spirit and in truth." ²⁵ The woman said, "I know that Messiah" (called Christ) "is coming. When he comes, he will explain everything to us."

²⁶ Then Jesus declared, "I, the one speaking to you—I am he." ²⁷ Just then his disciples returned and were surprised to find him talking with a woman. But no one asked, "What do you want?" or "Why are you talking with her?" ²⁸ Then, leaving her water jar, the woman went back to the town and said to the people, ²⁹ "Come, see a man who told me everything I ever did. Could this be the Messiah?" ³⁰ They came out of the town and made their way toward him (John 4).

© Gajus/Shutterstock.com

In this story, Jesus, a Jew, is interacting with someone from two totally different disfranchised cultures: women and Samaritans. Certainly, the comment of Jesus' disciples in seeing him talking to a Samaritan indicates the prejudice toward Samaritans. Additionally, in Jesus time, women were largely marginalized within Jewish culture. Rabbinic literature of the time demonstrates that women were depreciated, and Samaria was largely avoided by devote Jews (Brand, England, & Draper, 2003).

Historians have noted that the woman's drawing at the noon hour is not the usual hour for that chore to be performed and is an indication that she is either purposefully avoiding others and/or is an outcast of her society. Certainly, the allusion to her having multiple husbands is an allusion to her moral character and may imply that she was a prostitute (Kaufmann, 2013).

Jesus' interaction with this woman at the well is much like the interaction between a counselor and a client when there are differences of values, beliefs, and cultures. Like Jesus, our duty is to go to our client's world, for the good of our client, for the purpose of their growth and redemption. It is a path that begins with grace, unfolds with grace, and ends with grace. It is an attitude, belief, and practice that is embodied by Philip Yancey's (1997) definition of grace: "Grace means there is nothing I can do to make God love me more, and nothing I can do to make God love me less."

Name: _____   **Date:** _____

Scenario 3:

Bennie is a counselor in an outpatient setting. He has been seeing Isabella, a 34-year-old Hispanic female who, at start of care, stated to Bennie that she wanted to talk about her sadness about not being married. Isabella reveals to Bennie that she continues to live at home with her parents. Bennie encourages her to move out of her parents' home explaining to her that it is immature to continue to live with her parents at her age. How has Bennie violated the principle of beneficence?

5 Justice

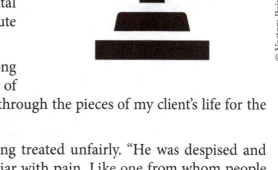

Turn on the news on any given evening and you are hit by the injustice of a fallen world. No one can get through life without being the victim of injustice. If you have ever been a victim of injustice, then you know that sharp, penetrating, pain.

The American Counseling Association (ACA, 2014, p. 3) defines justice as, "treating individuals equitably and fostering fairness and equality." In so defining justice, the ACA recognizes the inequality of our society in having equal and just access to mental healthcare and the everyday resources that contribute to our well-being.

© Vectors Point/Shutterstock.com

To foster someone, or something, is to come along side to work for their benefit. This is the essence of counseling. I come alongside my client as we walk through the pieces of my client's life for the good of my client.

God knows something about injustice and being treated unfairly. "He was despised and rejected by mankind, a man of suffering, and familiar with pain. Like one from whom people hide their faces he was despised, and we held him in low esteem," writes the prophet Isaiah (Isaiah 53:3). "My God, my God, why have you forsaken me?" Jesus cries out on the cross, and in so doing, epitomizes the cry of our every human soul who has suffered for wrongs you did not commit (Matthew 27:46).

To promote justice for the benefit of my client requires action on my part. Jesus was a man of action who purposely went to the worlds of the disenfranchised by dining with the unrighteous, healing outcasts liked lepers, defending and forgiving marginalized women, and mingling with those considered less than. His actions unnerved the status quo.

Luke records the story of Jesus being challenged by "an expert in the law" regarding the responsibility to extend God's love to others. In response, Jesus unfolded this parable:

> 30 In reply Jesus said: A man was going down from Jerusalem to Jericho, when he was attacked by robbers. They stripped him of his clothes, beat him and went away, leaving

him half dead. [31] A priest happened to be going down the same road, and when he saw the man, he passed by on the other side. [32] So too, a Levite, when he came to the place and saw him, passed by on the other side. [33] But a Samaritan, as he traveled, came where the man was; and when he saw him, he took pity on him. [34] He went to him and bandaged his wounds, pouring on oil and wine. Then he put the man on his own donkey, brought him to an inn and took care of him. [35] The next day he took out two denarii[c] and gave them to the innkeeper. 'Look after him,' he said, 'and when I return, I will reimburse you for any extra expense you may have.' [36] 'Which of these three do you think was a neighbor to the man who fell into the hands of robbers?' [37] The expert in the law replied, 'The one who had mercy on him.' Jesus told him, "Go and do likewise" (Luke 10).

© Dmytro Zinkevych/Shutterstock.com

In choosing his characters for this story, Jesus is making an important point. He is clearly stating to the religious leaders of the day that justice, and resources that come with justice, need to extend to all, regardless of their differences in race, religion, beliefs, and values.

As a counselor, you will have many clients who have been repeatedly "passed by on the other side." Instead of passing by, justice compels me to stop, look, listen, and immerse myself in the experience of my client. It requires me to enter the trauma of my client's world. It requires me to pick up the cross of my client, as Simon of Cyrene, helped carry the cross of Christ (Luke 23:26). Finally, it requires trust in God. I must trust God that helping my client carry the cross through what feels like a journey unto death for my client is a journey to life. For, as the writer of Hebrews (11:2) reminds us, "For the joy set before him he endured the cross, scorning its shame, and sat down at the right hand of the throne of God."

Name: _____   Date: _____

Scenario 4:

Tess has just become certified in Eye movement desensitization and reprocessing (EMDR) and is anxious to incorporate it into her practice with clients who have been diagnosed with Post-traumatic stress disorder (PTSD). One of Tess' clients is Marvin, a Vietnam veteran who has been diagnosed with PTSD. From what Tess has learned, Marvin would be appropriate for EMDR. However, because Marvin frequently misses his appointments, and has demonstrated a pattern of not complying with previous therapy suggestions, Tess decides to "not waste time on something he will get nothing out of." How has Tess violated the principle of justice?

6 Fidelity

Fidelity is the proof of love. Being faithful to someone or something is the evidence that you have loved from deep convictions. And like God's character of immutability, being faithful is never contingent on another. I decide to become and remain faithful regardless of your response. This is especially true as a professional counselor as my commitment to my client is not based on his/her commitment to me.

God knows something about faithfulness to those who, either from unwillingness or inability, are unable to remain faithful. "If we are faithless, he remains faithful, for he cannot disown himself," writes Paul (II Timothy 2:13). The faithfulness of God is further revealed in the book of Hosea, where God paints a picture of remaining faithful even when one is betrayed.

Regardless of my willingness or ability to remain faithful, God remains faithful to me. This is seen in the story of Abraham and Sarah:

> The LORD appeared to Abraham near the great trees of Mamre while he was sitting at the entrance to his tent in the heat of the day. 2 Abraham looked up and saw three men standing nearby. When he saw them, he hurried from the entrance of his tent to meet them and bowed low to the ground (Genesis 18:1-2).

The purpose of God's visit was to promise Abraham and Sarah that they would have a child. Then one of them said, 'I will surely return to you about this time next year, and Sarah your wife will have a son' (verse 10).

In spite of this promise, Sarah responds with less than belief.

> Now Sarah was listening at the entrance to the tent, which was behind him. 11 Abraham and Sarah were already very old, and Sarah was past the age of childbearing. 12 So Sarah laughed to herself as she thought, "After I am worn out and my lord is old, will I now

have this pleasure?" ¹³ Then the Lord said to Abraham, "Why did Sarah laugh and say, 'Will I really have a child, now that I am old?' ¹⁴ Is anything too hard for the Lord? I will return to you at the appointed time next year, and Sarah will have a son." ¹⁵ Sarah was afraid, so she lied and said, "I did not laugh." But he said, "Yes, you did laugh."

Sarah's chuckled response revels her disbelief and her contempt. She has long since given up hope in her desire to have children and she has long since given up on the goodness of God. Yet, God remains faithful to her, in spite of her seething anger and disappointment in God.

One of the most difficult tasks as a counselor is to bear the hopelessness and anger of a client. Life's disappointments are often difficult to bear over time and clients drag these burdens into their relationship with the counselor. No truer words have been spoken when Paul writes,

> We know that the whole creation has been groaning as in the pains of childbirth right up to the present time. Not only so, but we ourselves, who have the first fruits of the spirit, groan inwardly as we wait eagerly for our adoption to sonship, the redemption of our bodies (Romans 8: 22-23).

We all groan under the burden of a world where there is something wrong with everyone and everything. Our hearts tell us we were created for something better and more, but our eyes see it from afar. In spite of this state, fidelity requires I remain faithful to my client. To do so, I must remain hopeful in the goodness and faithfulness of God. For as Paul writes, "¹² For now we see only a reflection as in a mirror; then we shall see face to face. Now I know in part; then I shall know fully, even as I am fully known" (I Corinthians 13:12).

© frankie's/Shutterstock.com

Name: _____   **Date:** _____

Scenario 5:

Todd is marriage and family therapist in private practice. He has a long waiting list of clients wanting to get into his practice. As part of his consent form, Todd lays out that each client sessions runs 1 hour. Though Todd is quite successful he is frequently late to his appointments with clients and often runs over the session hour. How has Todd violated the principle of fidelity?

7 Veracity

Life, for everyone, is predictably unpredictable and many of our clients come having had the rug of their lives suddenly pulled out from underneath them. Unpredictability within the context of an intimate relationship is perhaps the most unnerving of all.

This is where veracity becomes important. The ability to be faithful is paramount in establishing with your clients that you are the safest person in their world of chaos. But veracity is more than something I do for another, it must be who I am with myself, God, and then others. It is my very character.

© ilkercelik/Shutterstock.com

The Biblical narrative is a narrative of a faithful God who remains faithful even to those who do not remain faithful to Him. He is the constant, the stake in the ground that never moves. His immutability is our one constant in life (apart from the old saying of taxes and death)!

"Know therefore that the LORD your God is God; he is the faithful God, keeping his covenant of love to a thousand generations of those who love him and keep his commandments" (Deuteronomy 7:9). "If we are faithless, he remains faithful, for he cannot disown himself," Paul reminds us (II Timothy 2:13).

Nothing is more disarming and comforting than the faithfulness of another human being who remains faithful, even when I am unfaithful. John, chapter eight, reveals the faithfulness of Jesus:

> [3] The teachers of the law and the Pharisees brought in a woman caught in adultery. They made her stand before the group [4] and said to Jesus, "Teacher, this woman was caught in the act of adultery. [5] In the Law Moses commanded us to stone such women. Now what do you say?" [6] They were using this question as a trap, in order to have a basis for accusing him. But Jesus bent down and started to write on the ground with his finger. [7] When they kept on questioning him, he straightened up and said to them, "Let any one of you who is without sin be the first to throw a stone at her." [8] Again he stooped down and wrote on the ground. [9] At this, those who heard began to go away one at a time, the

older ones first, until only Jesus was left, with the woman still standing there. [10] Jesus straightened up and asked her, "Woman, where are they? Has no one condemned you?" [11] "No one, sir," she said. "Then neither do I condemn you," Jesus declared. "Go now and leave your life of sin."

The state of the Pharisees' hearts is telling when John relates their motivation for presenting this woman to Jesus. They did not care about her. She is simply a pawn in their theological debate. They only cared about being right and proving Jesus wrong. They were testing this new gospel of forgiveness that Jesus had been propagating. They hoped to shame Jesus by proving to the crowd that forgiveness was not sustainable in the "real" world where right and wrong mattered most.

But Jesus' question to the Pharisees, and whomever else might have been standing in the crowd, puts the shame back where it belongs: "Let any one of you who is without sin be the first to throw a stone at her," Jesus remarks. And weighing the consequences this dilemma poses, John writes of the crowds' decision, "At this, those who heard began to go away one at a time, the older ones first . . ."

It is true that with age comes wisdom. Most of us learn in the process of growing ourselves up that we have no stone to throw. All of our lives are filled with regrets—big or small. Thus, like the older witnesses in this story, we know we all need grace.

Jesus gives this woman just that—grace based not on her ability to keep the law of the land, but on his veracity. When the crowd had slinked away, his one-on-one approach to her is telling. [10] Jesus straightened up and asked her, 'Woman, where are they? Has no one condemned you?' [11] 'No one, sir,' she said. 'Then neither do I condemn you,' Jesus declared. 'Go now and leave your life of sin.' In one simple statement, Jesus holds out for this woman the very two things the apostle John said Jesus was all about: grace and truth. "[17] For the law was given through Moses; grace and truth came through Jesus Christ!" (John 1).

Name: _____   Date: _____

Scenario 6:

Amy is about to graduate from her counseling program. Amy very much wants to get an intern position as New Beginnings Psychiatric Hospital. Amy has heard that the hospital emphasizes Internal Family Systems (IFS) Therapy. Though Amy has only had one course in an overview of all family systems theories, she puts on her resume that she has extensive training in IFS. How has Amy violated the principle of veracity?

8 Bringing My Principles; Not Imposing Them

I began this book by briefly clarifying professional counselor identity and role. I discussed the differences between the profession of counseling and other helping professions. I explored the core principles of the profession of counseling: Autonomy, nonmaleficence, beneficence, justice, fidelity, and veracity and found that these principles were compatible with Christian doctrine.

I now revisit the question I raised at the beginning of this book: *"If I can't refuse to see clients, or refer clients, whose values conflict with my own, and I can't bring my own values to the professional relationship, then, as a Christian, can I, and how do I, work within those parameters?"*

Part of the answer comes from the profession of counseling. Experts in the field recommend a setting aside of one's personal values in order to attune to and understand both the client's world view and values. This process is known as "ethical bracketing" and is defined as:

> The intentional separating of a counselor's personal values from his or her professional values or the intentional setting aside of the counselor's personal values in order to provide ethical and appropriate counseling to all clients, especially those whose worldviews, values, belief systems, and decisions differ significantly from those of the counselor. When counselors deliberately set aside or bracket their personal values to honor their professional obligations, they help to avoid imposing those values onto clients and contributes to empowering clients to achieve their therapeutic goals (Kocet & Herlihy, 2014, p. 182).

The process of ethical bracketing is one that exhibits a deep respect for the personhood of the client. It implies the concept of client autonomy, that is, that clients have the right to make their own decisions. It also respects the value of beneficence, that is, acting for the good of the client, not the good of the counselor.

For the Christian counselor, the question arises, does Christian theology reflect the idea of setting aside one's personal values for the good of another? Certainly, Paul's words remind us of this concept:

> [19] Though I am free and belong to no one, I have made myself a slave to everyone, to win as many as possible. [20] To the Jews I became like a Jew, to win the Jews. To those under

the law I became like one under the law (though I myself am not under the law), so as to win those under the law. [21] To those not having the law I became like one not having the law (though I am not free from God's law but am under Christ's law), so as to win those not having the law. [22] To the weak I became weak, to win the weak. I have become all things to all people so that by all possible means I might save some. [23] I do all this for the sake of the gospel, that I may share in its blessings (I Corinthians 9)

To become like another is set myself aside and willingly enter the world of another . . . for another. It is a conscious choice that requires I empty myself so there is room for the other. Theologian Henri Nouwen (1975, p. 102) defines this process as hospitality:

> When we think back to the places where we have felt most at home, we quickly see that it was where our hosts gave us the precious freedom to come and go on our own terms and did not claim us for their own needs. Only in a free space can re-creation take place and new life be found. The real host is the one who offers that space where we do not have to be afraid and where we can listen to our own inner voices and find our own personal way to being human.

Setting aside my personal principles requires a deep-seeded belief in the power, goodness, and love of God. I must believe that God is in control of my client's life, even when my client's life is visibility careening out of control. It requires my trust that God loves and cares about my client far beyond my own ability and understanding and that, regardless of my client's choices, God remains faithful to my client.

The story of Jonah is the story of a man who struggled to empty himself for the good of those whose culture, morals, and values were very different from his own. When asked by God to go to the people of Nineveh, he, instead, ran away. But God was not deterred, and pursued Jonah until Jonah having spent several days in a very dark place, finally agreed. "[17] Now the LORD provided a huge fish to swallow Jonah, and Jonah was in the belly of the fish three days and three nights" (Jonah 1:17).

© Yafit/Shutterstock.com

It is understandable that Jonah did not want to go to Nineveh, as it was the capital of Assyria. The Assyrians and Israelites were old enemies. And, the Assyrians were known to be brutal to their enemies (Longman, 2014). Yet, God's love for the Ninevites was bigger than Jonah's understanding.

When Jonah finally relented and went to Nineveh to proclaim the message of God for the Ninevites, the Ninevites repented and turned toward God. Jonah's reaction was anger:

> ¹ But to Jonah this seemed very wrong, and he became angry. ² He prayed to the LORD, "Isn't this what I said, LORD, when I was still at home? That is what I tried to forestall by fleeing to Tarshish. I knew that you are a gracious and compassionate God, slow to anger and abounding in love, a God who relents from sending calamity. ³ Now, LORD, take away my life, for it is better for me to die than to live" (Jonah 4).

Jonah's response of anger is telling of his inability and/or unwillingness to let go of his values to create a space for someone different than himself.

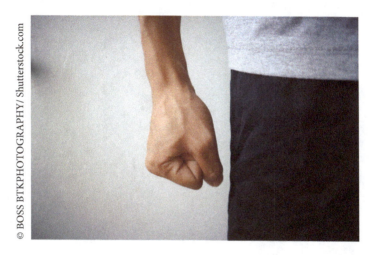

© BOSS BTKPHOTOGRAPHY/ Shutterstock.com

The story of Jonah also raises the question every Christian counselor must ask him or herself: Is it possible that my preconceived ideas and values can get in the way of God's work in my client's life? Ethical bracketing helps me get out of the way. It allows me to enjoy my client for himself, without the subtle demand to be someone different, better, more my idea of "well." It respects my client and is an indication of my ability to trust that God is powerful enough, loves completely enough, to work in my client's life. It is as Paul stated, "²⁰ Now to him who is able to do immeasurably more than all we ask or imagine, according to his power that is at work within us, ²¹ to him be glory in the church and in Christ Jesus throughout all generations, for ever and ever! Amen" (Ephesians 3).

Answers to Scenarios

Scenario 1

Answer: James has violated the value of client autonomy. Client autonomy requires that the client be given the right to make her own decisions regarding her treatment plan.

Scenario 2

Answer: Carter has violated the value of nonmaleficence. Carter has not recognized the importance of the counselor–client relationship to the client. In so doing, his refusal to help Jose has both shamed and hurt Jose.

Scenario 3

Answer: Bennie has violated the value of beneficence. Bennie demonstrates a lack of knowledge about the Hispanic culture in which it is common and acceptable for an older, single, female to remain at home until marriage. In so doing, Bennie has not acted for the good of his client, Isabella.

Scenario 4

Answer: Tess has violated the value of justice. In not offering the same opportunity as her other clients, Tess has not treated Marvin fairly or equally.

Scenario 5

Answer: Todd has violated the value of fidelity. In not honoring his appointment times with clients, he fails to keep his agreement as laid out in his informed consent form.

Scenario 6

Answer: Amy has violated the value of veracity. In falsely claiming extensive training, Amy is not being truthful about her qualifications.

References

American Counseling Association. (2014). *ACA code of ethics*. Alexandria, VA: Author.

Brammer, J. (2014, July 13). Kentucky set to license pastoral counselors to provide faith-based mental health services. *Lexington Herald Leader*. Retrieved from https://www.kentucky.com/living/health-and-medicine/article44497572.html

Brand, C., England, A., & Draper, C. W. (Eds.). (2003). *Holman illustrated bible dictionary*. Retrieved from https://ebookcentral-proquest-com.ezproxy.liberty.edu

Gale, A. U., & Austin, B. D. (2003). Professionalism's challenges to professional counselors' collective identity. *Journal of Counseling and Development*, *81*(1), 3+. Retrieved from http://link.galegroup.com.ezproxy.liberty.edu/apps/doc/A98694602/AONE?u=vic_liberty&sid=AONE&xid=8cce737a

Herlihy, B. J., Hermann, M. A., & Greden, L. R. (2014). Legal and ethical implications of using religious beliefs as the basis for refusing to counsel certain clients. *Journal of Counseling & Development*, *92*(2), 148–153. doi:10.1002/j.1556-6676.2014.00142.x

Kaplan, D. M., & Gladding, S. T. (2011). A vision for the future of counseling: The 20/20 principles for unifying and strengthening the profession. *Journal of Counseling and Development*, *89*(3), 367–372. doi:10.1002/j.1556-6678.2011.tb00101.x

Kaufmann, L. (2013). The woman at the well and the poetry of thirst. *Grace & Truth*, *30*(1), 11–19. Retrieved from http://search.ebscohost.com.ezproxy.liberty.edu/login.aspx?direct=true&db=lsdar&AN=ATLAiGEV170630000539&site=ehost-live&scope=site

Kocet, M. M., & Herlihy, B. J. (2014). Addressing value-based conflicts within the counseling relationship: A decision-making model. *Journal of Counseling & Development*, *92*(2), 180–186. doi:10.1002/j.1556-6676.2014.00146.x

Leahy, M. J., Rak, E., & Zanskas, S. A. (2016). A brief history of counseling and specialty areas of practice. In I. Marini & M. A. Stebnicki (Eds.), *The professional counselor's desk reference* (pp. 3–7). New York, NY: Springer.

Longman, T. (2014). *The Baker compact Bible dictionary*. Grand Rapids, MI: Baker Books.

Mellin, E. A., Hunt, B., & Nichols, L. M. (2011). Counselor professional identity: Findings and implications for counseling and interprofessional collaboration. *Journal of Counseling and Development*, *89*(2), 140+. Retrieved from http://link.galegroup.com.ezproxy.liberty.edu/apps/doc/A252289118/AONE?u=vic_liberty&sid=AONE&xid=439ec62b

Nouwen, H. J. M. (1975). *Reaching out: The three movements of the spiritual life*. New York, NY: Image.

Nouwen, H. J. M. (1993). *In the name of Jesus: Re ections on Christian leadership*. New York, NY: Crossroad.

Olthuis, J. H. (2001). *The beautiful risk: A new psychology of loving and being love*. Grand Rapids, MI: Zondervan.

Sullivan, W. F. (2014). *A ministry of presence: Chaplaincy, spiritual care, and the law*. Chicago, IL: University of Chicago Press. Retrieved from https://ebookcentral-proquest-com.ezproxy.liberty.edu

Tarvydas, V. M., Hartley, M. T., & Gerald, M. (2016). What practitioners need to know about professional credentialing. In I. Marini & M. A. Stebnicki (Eds.), *The professional counselor's desk reference* (pp. 17–22). New York, NY: Springer.

Walker, K. R., Scheidegger, T. H., End, L., & Amundsen, M. (2012, March). *The misunderstood pastoral counselor: Knowledge and religiosity as factors affecting a client's choice*. Paper based on a program presented at the 2012 American Counseling Association Annual Conference and Exposition, San Francisco, CA. Retrieved from https://www.counseling.org/resources/library/VISTAS/vistas12/Article_62.pdf

Wheeler, A. (2015). *The counselor and the law a guide to legal and ethical practice*. Alexandria, VA: American Counseling Association.

Yancey, P. (1997). *What's so amazing about grace?* Grand Rapids, MI: Zondervan.